Brain Vomit

Danny Tidmarsh

Presentation by *BookLeaf Publishing*

Web: www.bookleafpub.com

E-mail: info@bookleafpub.com

ISBN: 9789357212656

First edition 2023

Amie and our crazy zoo,

My love, my life, my inspiration

ACKNOWLEDGEMENT

First of all, I'd like to thank my partner in crime, Amie; without you, I don't know what I'd do. Thank you for supporting me and encouraging me to keep chasing my goals. You make me laugh when I want to cry. You have got me through the darkest nights and always remind me everything will be alright.

Thank you to my mum, Michelle, for proving that no matter how tough life gets, there is always light at the end of the tunnel. You have always been there to guide me and help me grow in so many ways.

My sister, Chantelle, you never fail to make me laugh. I am so proud of what you have achieved, and you will help shape so many lives through your teaching.

Thank you to my nan, who has always been just a phone call away. You have such a kind heart and are always there when needed.

Thank you to Miggy, my gran. You remind me that it doesn't matter what the rest of the world thinks; you have always allowed me to embrace my authentic self.

Thank you to my Dad for constantly pushing me to carry on. You taught me that when you put your mind to something, you can achieve it regardless of how difficult the journey may be.

Grandad, you are one of the strongest people I know. No matter how tough you may seem on the outside, you have a huge heart and have always supported us; thank you for everything. I never imagined at 22, I'd relate more to my Grandad than people my age, but I love that we can laugh about that.

I am lucky enough to say that we have a huge family, so I want to thank anybody who has ever believed in me and encouraged me to pursue my hopes and dreams.

I want to thank my closest friends, Beth, Carter, and Katie, for being there for me all these years and putting up with all my weird quirks and traits. You have always been there for me, and no matter how much time has passed, whenever we get together, it's like it was only yesterday.

Thank you to Luka, founder of Rebel Manifesto Aerial. I met you almost three years ago, and you have been such a huge inspiration to me. You have helped me reach new heights (quite literally) and have supported me in achieving things I never thought I could.

I wish I could name every person who has ever inspired me, made me feel less alone, or helped me in some way, but I'm sure the list would be longer than the book itself. I hope that everybody knows how much I genuinely appreciate every single person in my life and everybody who has ever taught me.

I am grateful to the Recovery and Wellbeing Academy; for providing psychoeducational courses free of charge which I have utilised and benefited from.

Finally a huge thank you to BookLeaf Publishing for allowing this dream to come true. I never thought I'd have my very own published book of poetry, but this challenge has allowed me to push past my comfort zone and go for it.

PREFACE

I know it's cliché, but it has always been a dream of mine to be an author someday. However, as a chronic procrastinator, someday never comes, so this 21-day challenge was a perfect motivator. If you're anything like me, you'll agree that signing up for anything that may take more than six months to complete sounds like a huge commitment, but signing up for 21 days feels manageable.

I find this humorous because it can take around 21 days to form a habit (obviously dependent on the habit), so if you can manage the 21 days, you will likely continue for longer. As somebody who has never really been able to imagine my future, I am immensely proud of myself for seeing this through. Writing this poetry has been a great achievement for me, and I hope to celebrate it being turned into a book.

I want to thank everybody who has helped me through this year, 2022 has been very challenging, and without the love and support from those around me, I may not have found the strength to write. During the last couple of months, I have been at my lowest points in a long time. This is due to a mixture of things, including anxiety, financial stress, physical health problems, and difficulties navigating my relationships with others, exacerbated by my chronic illness and mental health struggles.

I have noticed an inevitable shift in our culture throughout the year. While it feels as though it is every man for himself, every so often, some moments remind us that there is still love and light in the world. I want to share my appreciation of my incredible partner Amie, for always making me smile even when I am at my lowest or when my pain is at its worst. To Jo for being a good friend, listening to me when I need to get things off my chest, and telling me when I'm being stupid or stubborn and need to admit I'm in the wrong. And, of course, my family, for always trying their best to support me no matter how grumpy or stubborn I can be.

It is an important lesson to remember that anything can happen if you put in the work. There are 21 poems in this book, and I hope at least one will resonate with you. Reader, I appreciate you and wish you well on whatever your journey may be.

You

You make me feel like less of a burden
But it was all just so sudden
At times I process things so slow
You do more for me than you can ever know
Even when I am feeling so low

I love you so so much
You allow me to lean on you like a crutch
We really do have so much fun
It doesn't matter be it rain or sun
But when all is said and done

I will love you forever and a time
You never do expect a dime
I would never have enough money to pay
You care for me in such a way
That I can't even find the words to say

But just know this
The power of your kiss
And the way you hold my hand
Makes me feel safe on this land
So together we can make a stand

Chronic Stillness

My beautiful curious beast.

And yet you care for me the least.

You remind me I'm barely living.

Yet my loved ones are forgiving.

I try to carry hope but right now I cannot cope.

A life once lived I lost, at an unreasonably high cost.

I fear the more I feel this pain, I'm allowing you more power to gain.

My body feels like a heavy log and let's not even mention the brain fog.

Some words are better left unspoken but you have left me feeling so broken.

Sometimes you strip me bare, no comfortable clothes I can wear.

My mask has fallen now and for help, I must
ask.

I remember now that the past is past.

I can only hope this feeling does not last.

Rebel

Rebel is a place that feels like home
A place that makes me feel less alone
A place where magic happens every day
A place where it's okay to explore and play
A place full of people willing to support you in
every single way

Rebel gives people purpose
Who knew you could find so much at the Circus
Aerial Hoop, trapeze, strops, and more
You never know what's going to be in store
The hard work never stops

Rebel is a place where it's okay to make
mistakes
A place where you never have to be fake
You never need to fake a smile
Rebel teaches you patience, take a step before
you attempt the mile
I never knew aerial could be so versatile

When I first started I was full of anxiety
Now it's a place of familiarity
Aerial makes me feel so free
I never believed I could do it you see

Rebel is and always will be a huge part of my
journey

As humans, it's so easy to get inside our head
Anxiety gets the best of us and fills us with
dread
When you allow yourself to feel the fear and do
it anyway
Amazing things can happen here
You are always welcome at Rebel dear

Please listen and Act

Please hear me when I tell you I'm in pain.
Please stop making me fear I'm going insane.
Please stop flushing every attempt I make down
the drain.

Poke a quick needle in my vein but the results
are always the same.
If the blood tests are clear then there's nothing
you can do, please tell me why it is that you
train?
You push and push but no, I will not stay in my
lane.

My memory may be hazy but I am certainly not
lazy and don't you dare try to make me feel like
I'm crazy.
I deserve care, this is just not fair, why is it that
you stare when I tell you about my affair?
I deserve respect but all I get is neglect and then
you wonder why I turn and deflect.

I just want to know why it is that you lie,
Tell me I'm fine, go home and try.

I would have so much more respect if you were
able to reflect and just tell me the real answer is
that you do not know what is wrong inside.

I love you

I appreciate you.
I will love you through and through.
I hope you will see my point of view.
This year chronic pain has completely destroyed everything I knew.
Keep going, keep pushing, keep working, you will feel brand new.
Everybody claims they understand but in truth, there are very few.
Now I sit here and I am able to reflect and review.
I realise that I have outgrown the me you once knew.

Change

I wish I could tell you why I am feeling so
afraid.
Or why my reaction times are so delayed.
I hope you see what a huge impact this has
made.
I used to be able to do what I loved and as a
bonus I got payed.
I cannot tell you how many items I have mislaid.
Please do not allow my beautiful memories to
fade.
It feels so unwelcome, it feels like I have been
personally preyed.
I don't think you could ever understand how
much I feel betrayed.
You would never know how many doctors I
have had to persuade.
Or how many times I have complained.
You couldn't know how heavy that weighed.
I do not care if I have to disobey if it means that
I will be remade.
I feel so broken and frayed but I know I am due
an upgrade
because this beast has overstayed.
I almost got myself detained.

Time and time again I explained my truth, I am feeling so very drained.

But you couldn't allow me the truth that you couldn't find the unexplained symptoms that I have been pained.

But I will not be restrained for getting to this stage because I have been failed.

It was only through the information that I obtained.

That I have finally gained the aids I need to function again.

Dust

When I tell you you're so strong
You have fought for so long
Don't you dare tell me that I'm wrong

When I tell you I love you
I promise it is true
Don't ever believe we cannot make it through

You are my light
Now don't ever give up the fight
Don't allow the monsters to make you lose sight

We will make our mark
And be there to hold each other when it gets
dark
Don't ever lose your spark

This is so much more than lust
You must continue to have trust
Don't let our love turn to dust

Now sit with me and Breathe
It does not matter if you wear scars on your
Sleeve
Believe we can fight this and we will Achieve

Fear

Nights are always the longest
It is only the strongest
Who can understand what it is like
To fight throughout the night
And keep hoping to see the light

I know what it feels like to be afraid
But even still I would not trade
I would not wish anybody to suffer
I don't think it could get any rougher
And yet I will get tougher

You make it all sound so easy
But I am feeling so queasy
I know I have made mistakes
No matter how much I continue to ache
I will not less this break me

I know I will survive
I will learn to thrive
I have wept and wept
But I need to accept
I will walk this journey step by step.

Zoo

I went to the zoo today
A big thing, one might say
I even cooked dinner, by the way
I might be on to a winner

Things have been tough, you see
Really quite rough for me
But together, we have a plan
To once again find Dan

My head has been going too fast to handle
But sometimes, you have to slow down
Maybe light a candle
Hypersensitivity to every sound

Too hot, too cold, too loud
Don't even consider a crowd
I have been really struggling to live
My head feels like a sieve

But I am finally starting to see light
I know I still have to fight
I once again try to embrace nature
I remember I am a creator

Anxiety

Sometimes I can't control it,
I know you want me to but I just can't sit.
My chest feels as though I've been stabbed.
My throat as if it's been grabbed.
I keep spiralling over minor errors,
I can't describe the feeling of terror.
I know it's not rational.
Sometimes I can't control the panic,
I know it looks to you as though I'm manic.

Sometimes I might pace,
But please be mindful if I need space.
My mind is going so fast I can't even think;
my lips are so dry. Perhaps I need a drink.
Please do not tell me to calm down,
It feels as though I may drown.
I have been lost, but I know I can be found.
Could you tell me if you can't hear that sound?

Be kind to yourself

Be kind.
Find whatever it is that you need to find.

Give yourself what you need to succeed.
As humans, there is no need for greed.

Try to appreciate the tiny things,
Life will bring what it brings.

It is important to remember,
As we near the end of December.

It doesn't matter the amount,
It is the thought that counts.

Have faith that the ones you love,
Are watching you from above.

Know that they are proud,
I hope you tell yourself this out loud.

And for the ones that are here,
Never forget to hold them near.

Respect

One thing I have learnt,
Is that respect is earnt.
I know you may disagree,
But there is no guarantee.
Sometimes you have to accept,
That you won't always be correct.
Admitting you are wrong,
Never makes you any less strong.
Sometimes people grow colder,
If I say, I don't respect you more because you're older.
Age means nothing,
If you are not loving.
Do everything with kindness,
Otherwise, you act from a place of blindness.
I know for a fact,
As humans, we have an incredible ability to adapt.

Life doesn't stop

I find it funny how the word disabled,
is considered an offensive label.
When about one in five of our population
has had to suffer at the hands of discrimination.

Most people can't possibly understand
what it is like to live this way firsthand.
It is a funny thing having to struggle
while also having to learn to juggle.

You see, life doesn't just stop when you live in
pain,
I must explain myself again and again.
If you continue not to make time for yourself,
you will be forced into making time for your
health.

Mind Body Soul

I know I should always be kind,
but sometimes, it is too much for my mind.
Thoughts, memories, and trauma make me blind.
But I know that I need to try and leave the past
behind.

I know I don't have the best physique,
I feel so weary, so drained, so weak.
Many a time, I have been called a freak.
But I know that I am me, and I am unique.

I know I need to let go of control,
in life, I have but one goal
To find what feels right in my soul
I know that is what makes me whole.

Age does not matter

Who determined that somehow age correlates
with feeling?
People's reactions to others' suffering can be
quite revealing.
Why are humans more concerned with what
shouldn't be
instead of just healing?

I know we can be better; we never stop learning.

It does not matter if you are 15 or 45 years old.
Nobody else can determine what your soul can
hold.
Don't let anybody else decide or control,
Have trust in yourself and let the journey unfold.

Listen

If only you'd have looked enough to see,
the pain I held inside of me.

You might have noticed then and there,
because this life is truly unfair.

It sometimes feels as though you do not care,
or maybe you were not aware.

All my life, I have felt people stare,
"You're far too young to be feeling this way."

That's what they would all say.
I hope you don't mind, but if I may,

Only when people stop and listen,
Does the light finally begin to glisten.

One day, I'll finally be able to spread my wings.
And with that hope, it brings a feeling of new
beginnings.

Reflection

I think upon reflection,
I no longer fear rejection.
I fear that I am not trying hard enough,
Now I won't lie and say it isn't tough.
I have to remember I can control my anxiety,
It is such a big thing in today's society.
I know I am not alone.
I fear the unknown.
I know I am my own worst enemy.
I have always struggled with my identity.
I am taking the steps,
It is no quick fix; I know it is complex.
I am alive.
I know I can survive.

Demon

You sit on my chest
Like a weighted vest
Or round my neck like a scarf
But that's not even half
You help me in so many ways
One of the reasons I stay
When I'm in so much pain
I can't talk or walk
You do something that makes me smile
And stay with me for a while
When I cannot stop or have a panic attack
You climb on top of my back
You are a cat without fur
But you stay there and purr
You always help me through the night
When I'm filled with fear and fright
When I sit there and want to die
You make me remember why
I will not give up this fight.

We will not accept defeat

I know you don't see your light
And I know that you've had to fight
But this isn't for winning or losing
The outcome is our choosing

You have walked miles and miles.
I assure you this is no trial
I see the light behind your eyes
It pains me to see your sighs

It may be a pattern that repeats
But we will not accept defeat
Though right now, it may feel strange
We must accept this change

No matter how low
You continue to help me grow
I can feel it coming soon
Our love will only continue to bloom.

I hope

I hope that I can help one person grow.
With all the seeds that I sow.

I hope I can help one person learn.
With all the lessons I have learnt.

I hope I can help one person feel less alone.
With all the things that I have known.

I hope I can help one person feel brave.
With all the stepping stones that continue to
pave.

 I hope I can help one person believe.
With all the goals that I achieve.

I hope I can help one person continue.
With everything in me, I know you have it
within you.

Life is a Gamble

I think life is a gamble.
Either follow the rules or be the example.

You have the tools to succeed.
But the outcome is still not guaranteed.

Take care of your heart.
And don't be afraid to go back to the start.

Sow seeds of hope to help others grow.
Know it's okay sometimes to go with the flow.

All of us may have different goals.
You have to learn to nourish your soul.

It's okay if there are very few
who ever really get to know the real you.